Faithful Servant Series

Meditations for
Lay Eucharistic Ministers

Beth Maynard
Christopher L. Webber, Series ⅰ

MOREHOUSE PUBLISHING

Morehouse Publishing
P.O. Box 1321
Harrisburg, PA 17105
Morehouse Publishing is a division of The Morehouse Group.

Library of Congress Cataloging-in-Publication Data

Maynard, Beth, 1962–
    Meditations for lay eucharistic ministers / Beth Maynard.
        p.   cm. — (Faithful servant series)
    ISBN 0-8192-1770-0 (pbk.)
    1. Lord's Supper—Lay administration—Episcopal
Church—Meditations. I. Title. II. Series.
BX5967.5.M35 1999
242'.69—dc21
                        98-55966
                        CIP

Passages marked BCP are from The Book of Common Prayer.

Hymn lyrics are from *The Hymnal 1982*, copyright 1985 by The Church Pension Fund.

Printed in the United States of America

*Cover design by
Corey Kent*

Contents

"You Were Chosen"

Were you chosen to read this book? Perhaps it was given to you in a public ceremony or maybe it was handed to you with a quiet "you might like to look at this." Maybe, on the other hand, it reached out to you in a bookstore and said, "Buy me!" Many books choose us in such ways and this book is likelier to have done so than most. But however this book came to you, it almost certainly happened because you have also been chosen for a ministry in the church or for church membership. Perhaps you hadn't considered this as being chosen; you thought you decided for yourself. But no, you were chosen. God acted first, and now you are where you are because God took that initiative.

God acts first—the Bible is very clear about that and God acts to choose us because God loves us. And who is this God who seeks us in so many ways, who calls us from our familiar and comfortable places and moves us into new parishes and new roles? Christians have been seeking answers to that question for a long time.

Part of the answer can be found within the church. We come to know God better by serving as church members and in church ministries. God is present with us and in others all around us as we worship and serve. But there is always more, and God never forces a way into our hearts. Rather, God waits for us to be quiet and open to a deeper relationship.

And that's what this book is about. This is not simply a book to read but to use, in the hope that you will set aside some time every day for prayer and the Bible—and for this book. So give yourself time not only to read but to consider, to think about, to meditate on what you have read. The writers of these short meditations have been where you are, thought about their experiences deeply, and come to know God better. Our prayer is that through their words and experience and your reflection on them, you will continue to grow in knowledge and love—and faithful service—of this loving, seeking God.

— Christopher L Webber
  Series Editor

Acknowledgments

Just as one never really prays alone, one never really writes alone either. I am grateful to have been accompanied on this journey by people too numerous to name from the many parishes where I have worshiped, first as a layperson and now as a priest. Christ Church, Grace Church, St. Aidan's, Good Samaritan, St. John's, St. Paul's, St. Elizabeth's, St. Gregory's, Trinity, St. Gabriel's, Good Shepherd: Whether or not your specific stories are in this book, some of your life is.

I give thanks for Debra Farrington from Morehouse, who suggested I undertake this project, and for Christopher Webber and his helpful editing.

Mark Dirksen, my husband, is the sine qua non—of this, and of all else.

Introduction

Congratulations on your call to serve as a lay eucharistic minister (LEM). Perhaps you are just starting out, and this is the first thing you've ever really done for the church; or perhaps you've already grown used to holding this leadership position (and maybe several others as well). Either way, you have taken on an important ministry.

If your parish is a small one, the ministry of a LEM may be a central responsibility. It may mean that you have to appear at every major public celebration of the Eucharist, perhaps serving at two liturgies each Sunday. You may be the only parishioner who would accept this appointment, or you may share the LEM responsibilities with another person.

Being a LEM at a large church can be an entirely different experience. Perhaps the rector will have signed up fifteen or twenty volunteers, and your turn at the altar may come only once every couple of months. Two years later, at the coffee hours after you serve, people in the parish (who ought to know better) will probably still be remarking brightly to you, "Hey, I didn't know you were a LEM!"

But whether you belong to a small church or to a large one, or to something in between, you are sharing in a unique experience: that of serving in a defined, public lay ministry. Now, a ministry is a funny thing. It can be a wonderful opportunity for spiritual growth, or it can turn into a deadening job. Whatever ministry we're talking about, after doing it for a while, you can end up wiser, or you can end up disillusioned.

One of the ways to make sure that a ministry is less likely to deaden you is to learn how to listen to it; that is, to notice where God may be speaking in the events that make up your role. In that sense, this book will offer you a collection of examples: some ways in which some people have noticed God while serving as LEMs. If reading about them encourages you to do your own noticing, you will be making connections among your experiences and the Word that is Christ. This skill, sometimes called "theological reflection," can make a big difference in helping you to find meaning in your work—and in everything else, by the way.

A second means of nourishing yourself is to attend to your spiritual growth in ways that are neither totally divorced from the context of your ministry nor totally confined to it. If you pray only once a week with the altar party, as the procession is forming, you will soon find God seeming more and more distant at the rail. On the other hand, you may already have lots of "spirituality opportunities" built into your life; but if they do not invite you to connect with the Scriptures and the sacraments, they will probably give little enrichment to your ministry in Christ's church.

This book, then, will ask you to spend time on both these paths. It will open up some of the experiences many LEMs share and reflect on them. It will also suggest other ways to nourish the spirit, guided by the Bible and The Book of Common Prayer. And finally, it will invite you to think about the joys and challenges of ministry, as well as about how you might integrate them into the rest of your life.

Use this book and its meditations any way that works for you. Leave it in the bathroom or on your bedside table. Start your lunch hour with a page or two. Or just let it be a reminder that your own spiritual life deserves time and thought. Care for yourself, tend your own garden, and you will be better able to be a blessing to the people you see across the rail.

AT THE ALTAR

Like living stones, let yourselves be built into a spiritual house.

1 Peter 2:5a

The first time I stood behind an altar, I was too nervous to pay much attention to anything beyond not dropping the chalice. However, as I grew used to being in the chancel, I began to be able to focus on other, less mechanical things. One of those was to notice how different the church looked from the far side of the rail.

Sitting in my place in the pew, I had always enjoyed having a good view of the stained-glass window over the altar. When the sermon was boring or the liturgy was lackluster, that window could be my main spiritual nourishment for the day. Yet, after moving into the chancel, all that was behind me. My view changed. Instead of being made up mostly of art, polished brass, and organ pipes, the church turned out to be made up of faces.

As you look out from your own chancel, you may realize, as I did, how different those faces are. Some seem attentive, some fidgety, and others are wearing a specialized "I'm-in-church" expression that you can't interpret. There is a greater diversity in dress than what you notice when sitting in the middle of the congregation. The extremes of age are more obvious, and if there are only a few worshipers of a particular race, they stand out as well. From the chancel you can tell immediately: We have all kinds of people here.

Another kind of perspective is gained from the chancel vantage point too. For example, you notice who does not come up to receive. You notice when people have positioned themselves more or less alone, three pews from anyone else. You see if someone is huddled in the back or against a wall, divorced from the action. If something like this stands out to you suddenly when you look at the congregation, by all means pray about it. Who knows if the Spirit isn't pointing the individual out so that you can do just that? You may be the only one who will.

And, of course, from the chancel you can also see the joys. Whole families together in the pew for the first time in six months. Someone privately laughing at a joke in the sermon, or a parishioner with evident relish for the choir's offertory anthem. If you see those, pray about them as well. Thank God for their joy; they may forget to.

In my early days as a LEM, I used to miss gazing quietly at the stained glass over the altar. Eventually, though, I became grateful for the opportunity to view my parish from another perspective. The window I loved seemed pretty colorful, but the people were much more so.

...who made there, by his one oblation of himself once offered, a full, perfect, and sufficient sacrifice, oblation, and satisfaction, for the sins of the whole world.

BCP 334

If you serve at the altar long enough, you will see all kinds of mistakes made. Mini-disasters will be narrowly averted or, more often, not averted at all. Flies will dive-bomb the altar book and bees will fall into the chalice. There will be way too much wine. There will be no wine at all and instead two cruets of sparkling clear water. Two cruets of wine are another possibility, and especially interesting when the priest tries to get her hands washed from one of them. Sometimes an object will catch on fire. At least one acolyte will eventually faint, throw up, or have to stagger out in order to throw up somewhere else at the most solemn of moments. Somebody—and why not you?—will spill the wine. Maybe a few drops on the floor by the credence table, or maybe a big sodden mess all down the front of the senior warden's blazer.

Yet you will not get fired for this. In a healthy situation, no one will yell at the altar guild or embarrass the acolyte corps. Most clergy will laugh with you about it later. God will still love you, even as you stand there attempting to purge your chalice of a drunken, potentially consecrated bee.

Christians call this grace, and many of us don't really believe in it all that much. Somehow we just keep trying, impossibly, to present God with a perfect offering, without spot or blemish. An offering that needs no help to be acceptable. When people cannot laugh at their mistakes in the service, when a dropped cue (or cruet) gets treated like the end of the world, we have forgotten that the task of making a full, perfect, and sufficient sacrifice, oblation, and satisfaction was in Jesus' job description, not ours.

And so, perhaps God sometimes deliberately allows our mistakes. Perhaps he even enjoys confounding our liturgical efforts now and again in order to remind us that there's only one perfect offering, thanks, and it was made two thousand years ago on a hill outside Jerusalem.

The scribe Ezra stood up on a wooden platform… and beside him stood Mattithiah, Shema, Anaiah, Uriah, Hilkiah, and Maaseiah on his right hand; and Pedaiah, Mishael, Malchijah, Hashum, Hash-baddanah, Zechariah, and Meshullam on his left hand.

Nehemiah 8:4

One of my favorite things about year C is this reading, assigned for the Third Sunday after Epiphany. It describes Ezra's public promulgation of the Torah, held in about 445 B.C. for former Judean exiles who had returned to Jerusalem. Of course, this ceremony was important, and we should all remember it. However, what I really like best about the passage is its interminable lists of unpronounceable Hebrew names.

Things go about the same way each time this lection comes up in church. For a few verses, everything seems normal. But then the names begin. Congregants glance down curiously at their inserts and look back up with widened eyes. You see smiles forming on the faces of the choir. A snicker escapes from the acolyte bench. When the reader finally completes the list and goes back into the narrative, usually a palpable sense of relief floods the room. Whew. Who picks these things? That was really something, wasn't it? Whereupon we hear "Also…," and the next list abruptly begins, ticking off a total of thirteen Levites. Any congregation in which no one laughs at this point is probably asleep.

I have seen this lection printed with brackets and a few gentle editings that would allow a skittish lector to skip all the names. In my experience, however, usually readers insist on trying them and end up pulling it off quite creditably. As amusing as it can be to sit through twenty-six names of long-forgotten foreign religious leaders, there is something in us that knows we'd better read them. These names may have been as well known in their society as Billy Graham and Mother Teresa are in ours. And it is history: They were there, so they ought to get credit for it. We owe Hash-baddanah and Akkub and all the rest that much.

Even more, though, we read these names because we are like the person who recorded them. We do the same thing. We list, we tally who was there, we try to keep the memory alive. For the Easter flowers, for the All Saints'/All Souls' memorials, and for the Christmas greens, how long of a list of names goes in your church bulletin? Surely God did wonderful works in each of those lives; but already only some of them are still remembered. Many mean nothing to anyone besides the one great-niece who mailed in that five dollars. And in every holiday list, aren't there always a few names whose pronunciation has to be debated and verified with relatives?

We are a naming faith. We are a historical faith. The works of God in human lives are too numerous for us to remember them all, but we try. Sometimes all you can do is what the author of Nehemiah did: Just make the list, trusting that when other believers come upon it years later, they will, like us, do their best to read all the names.

Together met, together bound, we'll go our different ways.

Hymn 304

The big days, like Christmas Eve, bring high volume LEMing. The faithful just keep on coming, and you have to refill the chalice over and over from that festival flagon that is brought out only two times a year. Where are all these communicants arriving from? People who you normally see at the rail alone have suddenly sprouted relatives: blasé youth, happy aunts, tense siblings, nieces and nephews. What stories lie behind all these people? What lives are we suddenly intersecting?

Will one of them, fifteen years later, point to this communion as the moment that persuaded them to start coming back to church? Will another feel the combination of the music and the sermon and the taste of the wine coalesce into something like God's voice personally addressing them? "Ann, it's time to leave nursing." "Frank, I will strengthen you for the job that lies ahead."

And all the while we LEMs are thinking, as often as not, about minutiae: Should I go for a refill now, or wait one more rail? Is it time to reverse the purificator yet? Most likely I'll never hear about their precious moments with God. Or they about mine. After all, the minutiae don't always win. There are times when I simply know with a kind of calm assurance that Christ is in our midst. The arguments about the exact way that happens turn out to be irrelevant then. I know that

I am holding history in my hands—who we are and how we live. All that gives us being is in this cup and bread.

Yet these kinds of experiences, whether it's you or a communicant that has them, are sudden, vertical moments of realization. People's stories spread out from beginning to end in one direction, and your ministry as a LEM intersects with most of them running the opposite way. You rarely get the horizontal, the whole story, the before and after.

On summer Sundays, perhaps, when it's only the regulars, you may get to hear a horizontal tale or two. Yet at Christmas, people cross paths for one little moment at the communion rail, and then it's over. You will probably never know what kind of difference God made there, or for whom; and it is not your job to go around asking.

So all you can do is pause for a moment, as you set the empty chalice in place on the beautifully dressed altar. Stop and give the whole affair to God. Here we are, so many people, so many stories, our paths crossing without a clue. Whatever you would make of this, Lord, make of it. And thank you for bringing us here.

Two men went up to the temple to pray, one a Pharisee and the other a tax collector. The Pharisee, standing by himself, was praying thus, "God, I thank you that I am not like other people: thieves, rogues, adulterers, or even this tax collector."

Luke 18:10–11

My first experience of feeling like a eucharistic insider lasted about sixty seconds. At an informal liturgy where we had all been invited to gather in a circle around the altar, I happened to end up immediately to the celebrant's left. After we had all received, he was cleaning up (I had not yet learned the term "ablutions") and turned to me with the cup. I guessed from this gesture that he needed help to consume the rest of the wine. Feeling flattered to be asked, I took the cup and drank again. But I didn't know that usually anyone doing this would be expected to finish the contents and return an empty chalice to the celebrant. So after having taken a substantial swallow, I handed the cup to the next person, who drank, and (not knowing the drill any more than I did, apparently) passed it along as well.

That chalice made it about halfway around the circle before the wine gave out. The blood of Christ… again. Did you enjoy yours? Care for some more? The inflated notion of being a eucharistic insider was replaced by the dawning realization that this definitely was not supposed to be happening.

I was pretty new to Christianity then, but even regular churchgoers aren't necessarily familiar with everything that might be expected of us. Knowing a particular custom measures not your seriousness or your commitment, but probably just whether or not you happen to know that custom.

For some reason, however, it is often minor customs that attract major energy. People can come to feel deeply gratified by having learned, say, which altar candle to put out first. (That would be the gospel side, which is technically obsolete—but still occasionally used—church code for the left. There was once a good reason for this terminology.) I sometimes forget the proper order of candles myself, and whenever I did so in one parish, a particular gentleman would take that opportunity to favor us with an audible gasp of horror.

So, he was like me standing in that circle, thinking "insider"; he was like all of us, because basically we like to be right, don't we? Maybe we grasp our customs so tightly because they give us the chance to feel right, to preen and display our superior knowledge. Sooner or later we quite naturally congratulate ourselves, "I am an insider. I know the correct way." And then, perhaps, we may continue, "Thank God I am not like all those Philistines who pass the chalice twice around the circle and extinguish the Epistle candle first." By the time we get to that sentiment, though, one hopes we might be reminded of a parable. Luke 18, I think it is. Something about a Pharisee.

For in the night in which he was betrayed, he took…

BCP 342

…a chalice that was not nearly as blindingly polished as the one I am about to pick up. How long did the altar guild work to get the silver this perfect? But it will be perfect only for roughly another ten seconds, because I am about to pick this chalice up, and then there will be a fingerprint on it. The surface will still reflect the lights over the altar, but a smear or two will be visible in the middle where my hands have held the bowl. The chalice was perfect, impeccably clean, but only until I picked it up.

As I move down the rail, offering people this cup of salvation, it will become even less perfect. Some communicants, instead of obeying the bulletin's discreet suggestion that they "gently guide the chalice to their lips," take the whole thing out of my hands and hoist it up as if it were a beer stein. I secretly like those people, but they put more fingerprints on the silver.

Many women do not blot their lipstick, so each of them leaves a pinkish smear on the rim of the chalice, not to mention on my purificator. The assistant rector told us at our LEM training that as long as we didn't actually let lipstick get on the embroidered cross in the center, everything would be all right. Well, of course I promptly let lipstick get on the embroidered cross in the center.

Every Sunday, it takes only a rail or two until the cup is dirtied with all kinds of evidence of humanity. This no longer blindingly polished chalice has been handled by all of us, with our pains and concerns and joys. If someone came to the church to dust for fingerprints, we would all be incriminated. Sometimes it seems to me that what's really imprinted on the chalice is the record of our lives. Whether or not the altar guild restores this chalice to the appearance of perfection after the service, all of their polishing will never be able to wipe that record away. God will remember us.

A corny old poster, often seen yellowing and curling from the bottom in youth fellowship rooms, asked: If you were put on trial for being a Christian, would there be enough evidence to convict you? Well, whatever else happens, my fingerprint is on this chalice.

LOOKING AT
THE BACKGROUND

The sacraments are outward and visible signs of inward and spiritual grace.

BCP 857

Whether you were confirmed as a child or as an adult, part of your preparation probably involved memorizing a list of the sacraments. Baptism and Eucharist, the two sacraments of the gospel, have pride of place. Then there are the five lesser sacramental rites that have evolved under the guidance of the Spirit: holy matrimony, confirmation, ordination, reconciliation, and anointing for healing.

These seven (or as one priest calls them, the big two and the little five) do not, however, exhaust the sacramental possibilities in God's creation. In medieval times there were much longer lists of sacraments, varying from theologian to theologian, and who's to say that they weren't closer to the truth than our neat list of the standardized seven? For example, isn't the church itself an outward and visible sign of an inward and spiritual grace? And couldn't those words describe Jesus as well? In a sense, Christ and his church are sacramental realities even more fundamental than baptism and Eucharist.

Also, there are a thousand lesser ways in which outward and visible things communicate the unseen to us. A note from your beloved, a delivery of flowers for no special reason, a mother's cool hand rubbing the back of a feverish child—is God's grace absent from these? The fact that God has specially promised, covenanted to infuse seven particular rites with grace does not prevent God from flooding the rest of the material world with grace as well.

Sacraments are part of our church practice because the sacramental principle is written into creation. The more we learn to notice the inward and spiritual graces concealed beneath the outward and visible signs of daily life, the more the sacraments should mean to us. And the more we learn to love the sacraments, the more we should come to love creation, our bodies, and our world. As Teresa of Avila said, anyway, it's all grace.

He was the Word that spake it, he took the bread and brake it, and what that word did make it, I do believe and take it.

Hymn 322

Memorizing the words of administration is one of those tasks that have to be done. The body of Christ, the bread of heaven; the blood of Christ, the cup of salvation—those are easy enough, if you're scheduled only for Rite II. But what about the long one, the Elizabethan one: "The Blood of our Lord Jesus Christ, which was shed for thee, preserve thy body and soul unto everlasting life. Drink this in remembrance that Christ's Blood was shed for thee, and be thankful"?

This speech, which is fairly tricky to recite as you're both walking and administering, has a complex pedigree. In the 1549 English Book of Common Prayer, the priest recited only the first sentence to each communicant. But the people who had been reading that era's Protestant theology criticized those words as too Roman Catholic. The body of Christ, the blood of Christ: It sounded so objective, almost magical, almost superstitious. Wasn't the faith of each worshiper important?

So in the revised Prayer Book of 1552, there were new, reformed words of administration: The celebrant pronounced only the second sentence, which emphasizes the attitude of the person at the rail. Each action verb refers to the communicant: Drink this; be thankful. But this, too, was criticized as neglecting the reality of God's action in the sacrament.

It was not until Queen Elizabeth I and the 1559 book that our tradition had the idea to put both sentences together. "The Blood of our Lord Jesus Christ, which was shed for thee, preserve thy body and soul unto everlasting life. Drink this in remembrance that Christ's Blood was shed for thee, and be thankful." Both ways of seeing the issue can find a home in that text. And however each of us understands what is happening as we offer the consecrated elements to our friends and enemies, these are the words the church still gives us to say in Rite I. They stretch back well over four hundred years, and they are as inviting today as ever.

As you walk down the rail, then, you balance more than just a chalice and purificator. As you bend to the height of each communicant, you offer words that themselves balance and accommodate different ways of encountering Christ. "The blood of Christ," you remind us; "take this in remembrance." In reciting these words, you help us Episcopalians to carry out what may be one of our special vocations: to keep on making room for people in all their ways of believing.

I am wiser than the elders, because I observe your commandments.
Psalm 119:100 (BCP)

Until about twenty-five years ago, the Episcopal practice was that children had to be confirmed (or "ready and desirous" thereof) in order to be eligible to receive communion. This rule established a rite of passage for youngsters that people came to care about deeply. And they still do, at least in some parishes, even though the 1979 Prayer Book comes down quite clearly on Baptism being the sole requirement for admission to communion.

Now, there is an explanation commonly given for this practice, but it actually arose long after the practice it is supposed to be explaining. Historically, withholding communion from the unconfirmed dates back to the thirteenth century, when an English archbishop decided to improve his country's abysmally low confirmation statistics. Taking a pragmatic route, the archbishop effectively excommunicated everyone of any age who had not yet been confirmed. If you wanted to receive the body and blood of Christ, you had to see him first.

A clever response to embarrassing parochial reports. And it worked: Confirmation numbers jumped. But you rarely hear this history mentioned in discussions of the issue. The nearly universal Episcopal explanation for denying communion to baptized children was, "The young people have to understand what they're doing before they are ready to receive." Has the Sunday school been adequately instructed? Do the children know enough about the Eucharist yet? These questions express a genuine concern, but one might respond by asking whether any of us can claim to know enough about it. And is it really formal instruction that we trust to teach us best here, in the realm of love and grace?

Whenever I hear someone argue for sending children away from the table empty-handed, until they can clear some intellectual hurdle, I remember a little girl of my acquaintance. She was certainly too young to "understand" the sacrament, in the sense most mean that term. She attended a Christian preschool sponsored by a denomination for whom the Eucharist was an occasional ceremony, not a weekly focus. Her teacher was rather alarmed by this child's evident excitement about studying communion in Sunday school and asked her what such a complicated ritual could possibly mean to her at her young age. "Well, I don't know how it works," the little girl said seriously. "But when we give it to the priest, it's bread. And when she gives it back, it's Jesus."

Shall we be honest? I doubt I understand it any better than that, really. I just use longer words.

When you come together, each one has a hymn, a lesson, a revelation, a tongue, or an interpretation. Let all things be done for building up.

1 Corinthians 14:26

Our English word "liturgy" comes from a Greek term meaning public works: major projects on which people from the community cooperate. Building a town hall, paving a highway, erecting a memorial to a beloved leader—in the original sense of the word, these were liturgies. Worship in the Episcopal Church illustrates this definition, because everyone is expected to participate according to the gifts God has given them. Our service is not a spectator sport, but a group effort.

So that we can contribute as the Prayer Book invites us, we learn our parts: words, gestures, music. In some places, most of these things may be printed in the bulletin; in others, we may be asked to find the right page in the book ourselves. In some places, instructions about when to stand or sit or kneel may be given; in others, we may be asked to observe what those around us are doing.

You will hear complaints that expecting the congregation to participate in this way is not adequately user-friendly. Some will speculate that newcomers are being alienated by a service that asks them to do more than watch. And indeed, there may be a place and time to offer more "seeker-sensitive" events, which presume no prior knowledge of the Christian tradition and help the unchurched ease into our liturgy.

But however people learn, the intention of all liturgical churches is that eventually we do learn. If we are mounting a public work, obviously that responsibility needs to be shared publicly, divided among all present. When this happens, there is a palpable sense of flow, of interdependence, of ease. Perhaps you have already experienced this sense in your work as a LEM. If you have, you know that it does not come about by accident; it comes when all are taking wholehearted responsibility for exercising their gifts.

Yes, it takes some time and effort to learn how to offer the conscious, intentional participation in the liturgy that our church expects of its laity. But it also takes time to learn to Rollerblade, to make love, to cook a good meal. Most worthwhile things take time. Sure, watching the Rollerblader, sniffing the soup, or being a spectator at worship may be less work. But isn't it also less rewarding?

It is a most invaluable part of that blessed "liberty wherewith Christ has made us free," that in his worship different forms and usages may without offense be allowed.

BCP 9

Some churches vest their LEMs, and others don't. Not surprisingly, both offer good rationales for their customs. If your parish dresses its LEMs in cassock and surplice or in an alb, people will tell you that these vestments symbolize being clothed in Christ. Others will explain that they are intended to make economic and class distinctions invisible. These are good explanations, but they probably will not prevent a third group from contending that vesting anyone at all is pompous and archaic.

If LEMs at your parish simply come forward in street clothes, you will hear the explanation that this practice creates a sense of greater accessibility and genuineness. Others will tell you that it symbolizes that you do not have to become someone else or muster an idealized presentation of yourself in order to serve God. These are good explanations, but they probably will not prevent a third group from contending that street clothes in the sanctuary are distracting and irreverent.

One parish I've seen dresses LEMs the same as acolytes, while a second carefully distinguishes between the two by color of cassock. A third congregation positions two unvested LEMs at the altar throughout the entire eucharistic prayer. Your church may have yet another practice. There are so many different ways to do things at worship, and every one of them communicates something. In fact, as the examples above illustrate, they can communicate several things at once.

Dress is only the beginning. Where do the acolytes sit, and how do their bodies look as they do it? When people bow, is it free and natural, or cramped and hurried? How does the altar draw the eye? What is the building itself saying about God? If you have spent many years in the same parish, you may never have thought about such questions: This is just how the church looks. We've always done it that way.

But in the environment of liturgy, there are more customs than absolutes. No matter what practice is under discussion, other people do it differently. So you may learn a lot from trying to see your parish's "forms and usages" with fresh eyes. Things are being communicated by whatever it is you've always done, and it can be very worthwhile to bring those things to consciousness. After some time spent reflecting on your parish's current practice, you might end up suggesting a change. Or you might not. But either way, you will have gained a new perspective, one that will deepen your participation in any kind of corporate worship. Take it with you to church and let it enrich your prayer.

And here we offer and present unto thee, O LORD, our selves.

BCP 336

Over the past decades, it has become common to speak of the Eucharist as having a fourfold action: taking, blessing, breaking, and giving. We see this series, as well as hear it recited, in every Eucharist: The elements are taken up just as Christ took bread the night before he died for us; the Great Thanksgiving is prayed by the celebrant on behalf of the assembly; the bread is broken at the fraction as we proclaim, "Alleluia, Christ our Passover is sacrificed for us"; and the elements are distributed to all the baptized persons present.

You can notice this series in other places as well; it is not confined to the sacrament of the altar. Any offering to God will display a similar pattern, and you can even use it as a structure for prayer about your own life and ministry. For example, you might look for this structure in your own calling to serve as a LEM. The taking happened as the church selected and designated you for a special ministry. Through licensing and commissioning, your ministry was blessed. But there also had to be sacrifice: time to learn, the pain of making mistakes, giving up a weekend trip you had planned, coping with teens who were digging in their heels about not going to church the first day you served. In some small (or perhaps not so small) way, there was a breaking. And then, the offering that had been taken, blessed, and broken—you, your ministry—is distributed to the people.

What might happen if you were to make that action more explicit in your prayer life? You could ask God to take you and put you to use, to bless more profoundly and break more generously whatever you offer. Tell God, if it's true, that you want more grace to be given to Christ's people through you. If you begin honoring that fourfold action and trying to recognize and extend it in this way, you will find it deep enough to hold all your aspirations.

Is this a grandiose way of speaking about a little volunteer slot? Perhaps. Your experience may seem an ordinary thing, hardly worth such theological analysis. But then, so much seems that way when you look on the surface. A baby in a manger. A little water poured on someone's head. If we brush off the claims of significance, determined to perceive only the ordinary, that's what we'll perceive. If we seek sacred truths, things will begin to open up their depths to us. Taken and blessed, broken and given—after all, even when Jesus did it, it was only a bit of bread.

INSIGHTS
FROM SCRIPTURE

For as in one body we have many members, and not all the members have the same function, so we, who are many, are one body in Christ, and individually we are members one of another. We have gifts that differ according to the grace given to us.

Romans 12:4–6a

Because you are a LEM, this means (I hope) that someone identified in you gifts for this ministry: perhaps characteristics such as a sense of liturgical presence, an affinity for public worship and the sacraments, an ease at sharing your faith through public visibility. In your own congregation, there may be specific other gifts that make sense for LEMs as well.

If this ministry matches well the gifts that God has given you, you stand a greater chance of finding it fulfilling, and your community stands a better chance of experiencing it as a channel of grace. As you continue serving as a LEM, you may see your ministry more and more as graced, noticing God's gentle workings through you. And you may become interested in exploring the topic of spiritual gifts.

There exist various inventories that can help Christians discern what their gifts from God are, and it's usually worth taking one of them. You may discover the Spirit inviting you to see yourself in new ways, to experience God in a different context than you have before. However, there's a certain clinical feel to those inventories; they can give the mistaken impression that a spiritual gift is something you either have or you don't, as unambiguous as, say, owning a motorcycle. That your gift is just that: yours, a personal possession.

In reality, spiritual gifts are much more fluid and mysterious. A spiritual gift is a manifestation of grace in a local situation, something that God is offering God's people through you. It probably fits in with your character and personality, but it can also call you beyond yourself. Some of these manifestations of grace are so undramatic that we have to be reminded that grace is at work. Others, in our culture, seem unusual enough that people huddle for nervous discussions when reports arise that somebody in the next parish over has been exercising one of them.

In either case, the grace is given for the common good. Since gifts are bestowed within a community, they are meant to contribute to that community. The Christ who dwells within the body wants to help us, the members of that body, serve and love in his name, and so he sends his people gifts. Some of them are meant to be delivered through you.

And when Jesus had been baptized, just as he came up from the water, suddenly the heavens were opened to him and he saw the Spirit of God descending like a dove and alighting on him. And a voice from heaven said, "This is my Son, the Beloved, with whom I am well pleased."

Matthew 3:16–17

I once found a pair of grade-school children whom I had baptized a few months earlier gathered in our church nave with several of their Sunday school classmates. They were on tiptoe, peering into the font and miming the gestures of baptism. They poured and splashed and cupped in their hands imaginary water, all the time explaining to an unbaptized preschooler, "This is where it happens. You should do it. It's neat."

I don't know whether Jesus ever brought disciples to the Jordan to witness the site of his baptism by John, but revisiting our own baptisms can be an important thing to do. It might even motivate us to say to others, "You should do it. It's neat."

Thinking and talking about the experience of baptism often occurs to adult converts, who have come to the waters from the increasing numbers of people who were "raised nothing." However, many other church members were brought up in an environment where they, along with everyone else in their families, unquestioningly received infant baptism and pubescent confirmation. It was expected; one did that sort of thing. People from this background may never have been back to look at that font, to plunge their hands into the water and ask: What really happened there? What is all the fuss about?

It's worth doing, because more and more we are grounding thought about our Christian lives in the truth of our baptisms. You will hear people refer to the baptismal covenant in The Book of Common Prayer, and you will have the opportunity to make a public renewal of your own vows at least a few times every year.

In baptism we die with Christ and rise to a new kind of life in him. We are flooded within by a Spirit of adoption, who gives us birth from God. Despite its biblical pedigree, some people are spooked by the phrase "being born again." Well, what else did you think was happening to you? The font, as some have said, is both a tomb, where your old self is buried, and a womb, where a new one is born. Passing through its waters gives us access, whether we consciously use it or not, to God's very life.

As you are brought into Christ, God's words to him become God's words to you. And if you have not ever heard them, stop and hear them now. "You are my beloved child. With you I am well pleased."

I will bless the LORD at all times; his praise shall ever be in my mouth.
Psalm 34:1 (BCP)

There is a list turning up in several publications this year that, I believe, is titled "100 Ways to Praise a Child." On a single sheet of paper in several different typefaces are printed brief exclamations of acclaim, things like: Way to go! You're super! What a great kid!

Children flower under such affirmation, and so do adults. Managers know that expressing appreciation for the employees they supervise will probably increase productivity and morale. Clergy try to remember to praise parish volunteers regularly. We cheer the members of our sports teams, and we affirm our friends as they take steps toward healthier lifestyles. It is easy to applaud when you can see your praise as a kind gift, encouraging someone who needs it. Way to go!

Maybe this is why so many people struggle with praising God. Certainly God doesn't require protection against low self-esteem. He's not liable to suffer from a bad at-bat or a spotty attendance record. We can't pat ourselves on the backs for affirming him. Sometimes we try to avoid the issue by collapsing praise into thanksgiving. If we can't get ourselves to tell the Lord how great he is, maybe we can just remember a few things God did for us. But it turns out that most of us aren't very good at that either. Did you ever notice how in the Prayers of the People a long list of intercessory concerns and names of the sick often contrasts with a brief, awkward silence after the bidding for thanksgivings?

And yet all through Scripture the voice of praise is never silent. The Psalms echo with shouts of acclaim, with vows never to stop extolling God. Corporate worship usually begins with praise. Study the lives of great Christians, and you'll notice doxologies and thank-yous sparkling at every turn. Monastics will tell you that praise is the great work of their lives. Open any hymnal, and you'll find myriad examples of adoration waiting to be sung.

Praise is woven through our tradition, first because it's true and second because we need to do it. God is everything we long for, more than we can ask or imagine, and we were made to say so. Saying so brings us to life. When we praise other people, they flower. When we praise God, we flower. And surely there are more than one hundred ways to do it.

Thus says the LORD: Stand at the crossroads, and look, and ask for the ancient paths, where the good way lies; and walk in it, and find rest for your souls.

Jeremiah 6:16

I heard a story the other day about an American who had an audience with a famous teacher of Buddhism, someone revered as a holy man. To Westerners, Eastern masters like that can seem exotic and numinous in a way that makes us question our own spirituality. Some of us may even begin to wonder if the religious traditions of the East have practices and teachings that are more profound than our own. Are we fated to fumble around being superficial at coffee hour while they are climbing the heights of mystical union? Have they got something we don't?

Apparently this American was feeling equally unsure of himself, because he asked the teacher for some spiritual guidance. What was his advice for Westerners who wished to become Buddhist? The reply was two words long: "Don't bother."

Upon questioning, the American learned that the teacher meant no slight to his own tradition. He was a Tibetan Buddhist and had benefited immeasurably from being formed by that heritage. To him the Dharma was certainly well worth bothering about; he had given his life to guiding people in their practice of it. It was just that he didn't see why Westerners would want to desert the richness of their own spiritual backgrounds. As far as this Buddhist master was concerned, all the spiritual depth anyone could need was right there in Christianity or Judaism, the religions that have taken root in Western culture. Why did we imagine that God could only be found by rejecting that culture and adopting someone else's? Stay where you were born, he advised; learn the practices of your own faith, and you will find what you are searching for there.

When you put it that way, he had a point. Yet many of us know people who now view the faith of their birth as superficial and will seek God only further afield. While there are indeed profound and authentic insights in other traditions, perhaps there is also a more prosaic reason why Western seekers turn East: the easiness of becoming complacent about the familiar. Christian language can be worn out for us through endless repetition—we hear it even in car ads. Soon we are lulled into saying, "So what; everybody knows this stuff." If we grew up with it, it must be old hat.

But if someone arrives robed in the vestments of a foreign land, speaking a language that sounds new and different, describing options we've never quite framed in those terms, we have to pay attention to follow the point. In short, we are likely to wake up. And is it any surprise that the ever-vigilant Holy Spirit seizes that moment of awakening, to whisper to us that perhaps this God business is real after all? The Spirit is whispering all the time, but we're too often asleep in church. If you can wake up to Christian language, you can discover that what that Eastern master said is true. All the enlightenment we need is right where we are.

After this I looked, and there was a great multitude that no one could count, from every nation, from all tribes and peoples and languages, standing before the throne and before the Lamb, robed in white, with palm branches in their hands. They cried out in a loud voice, saying, "Salvation belongs to our God who is seated on the throne, and to the Lamb!"

Revelation 7:9–10

If you ever doubt whether serving in the liturgy is an important job, read the book of Revelation. Not in too much detail, maybe, but read it. The vividness and vigor of the language in its passages about worship have inspired artists and musicians for centuries. Innumerable canticles and hymns have been born out of these pages.

Interestingly, while Revelation's descriptions of heaven are filled with passages like this, church per se has been abolished: There is no temple in the new Jerusalem. But this is because worship is so immediate and so integrated with our beings that we no longer need special places and times to remind us to do it. According to John, it turns out that without even having to check the rota, we are going to be worshiping forever.

Your reaction to that idea is probably a clue as to how effective your contemporary experience of worship has been. To some people, the prospect sounds boring. What's heaven like? "Angels playing on harps," they mumble disaffectedly, as if anyone with sense would opt instead for a ball game and a hot dog. Others, who have experienced the liturgy as a real locus of encounter with God, react differently. For them, worship is a place where they can voice their longing and love and pain. They have known what it is to enter a liturgical crucible and emerge having been forged into a new creation. They may even have come out of church once or twice saying to themselves, "I hope heaven is like this."

Probably there is no parish on earth where the liturgy does its work that effectively every week. But at least now and again, church ought to be helping us understand how kingdom worship could be so fulfilling that we won't need church anymore. Sundays ought, as the ancients used to say, to be giving us a foretaste of the heavenly banquet. Read about it in Revelation. And just imagine: They asked you to be cupbearer.

When you come together, it is not really to eat the LORD's supper. For when the time comes to eat, each of you goes ahead with your own supper, and one goes hungry and another becomes drunk. What! Do you not have homes to eat and drink in?

1 Corinthians 11:20–22a

The eleventh chapter of 1 Corinthians gives us some clues about how the Eucharist was celebrated in New Testament times. If you read the whole thing, you will find the familiar words of institution, just as we hear them in our Prayer Book. You will notice the reminder that this tradition was passed down to Paul, just as it has been passed down to us. You will also see something evident throughout Paul's letters, and that is how the Apostle regularly had to grapple with problems in local congregations. The Corinthians had apparently asked him for help with several issues, and here he addresses their questions about how to celebrate communion.

From Paul's answer, it seems that differences in social class were creating divisions in the Corinthian church. Some of the members were not of high birth and had little to commend them on worldly terms. Others, apparently, were people of some means. This latter group had developed the habit of showing up for the weekly community gathering and Eucharist carrying picnic suppers that they refused to share with the needy among them. Maybe they thought that the commoners simply wouldn't appreciate their goat cheese and chardonnay, or perhaps they dreaded having to accept another sparse cup of barbecued beans in return. Paul further says that they didn't even bother waiting for everyone to arrive before beginning.

As far as these Corinthians were concerned, everything was private property and personal preference until the formal liturgy began. You can imagine the exclamations: "Well, too bad; they're late! We're eating before it gets cold!" "It's none of your business what I'm having!" "Hey, get your own wine!"

It is not likely that many of our congregations are experiencing this exact problem. But maybe the Corinthian mindset is not totally foreign. After all, it really is hard to bypass, while inside the church, the markers of social class that have great power outside. Visitors in designer clothes will not immediately feel comfortable next to a parishioner who was outfitted at the thrift shop. Someone trained to appreciate Bach and Palestrina will have to make an effort to sing along with the simple gospel choruses beloved by so many people.

We bring more to church with us than we realize. Many of these things, like our talents and resources, need to be opened up and spread around generously. Some of what we carry, like our sins and prejudices, must be given away and laid on the altar. And surely we'd find ourselves toting all kinds of other things too, if we would stop to look. There is, I guess, nothing that we absolutely cannot bring into church with us. But when we get there, we'd better not count on being able to keep it for ourselves.

COMMUNITY AND COLLEGIALITY

All right, I have the chalice and the purificator. In the name of the Father, and of the Son, and of the Holy Spirit. Acolytes first. Wipe and turn. Don't fall off the step. The right half of the chancel, according to the rector, gets slightly less traffic at communion, so I am to begin by covering that side. I head down to the middle of the rail; the choir is already lining up to come forward.

Kathy, who taught Sunday school with me, kneels to receive the cup of salvation. It would really be more fitting for her to offer it to me. She always prays more than I do, and she surely knows the Bible better. Yet she holds the base of the chalice and guides it to her lips as if this were perfectly normal.

The choir returns to its stalls, and as the ushers step back and motion to the occupants of the front pew, I hear the hymn begin: "Father, we thank thee who hast planted thy holy Name within our hearts...." In a minute or two, I realize I forgot to wipe and turn. In fact, I've been forgetting for a while. How many times did I skip? Just stop now, clean the whole chalice rim. The senior warden and her husband both smile at me. I never imagined how much communication goes on at the rail. Be with me, Christ.

"Watch o'er thy Church, O Lord, in mercy; save it from evil, guard it still." Louise has told me what she is going through, and I give her the wine knowing that she knows that I know, and that I want this communion to help somehow. If I could do more, I would; but what more can I do than this?

Up comes Joe, who was yelling about the budget at annual meeting, who demanded we fire the church school coordinator to save money. I take a deep breath, because yelling bothers me, and because personally I would rather fire Joe if I could figure out something to fire him from. "Perfect it in thy love, unite it, cleansed and conformed unto thy will." Don't forget to wipe and turn. Well, Joe, God bless you anyway.

"As grain, once scattered on the hillsides, was in this broken bread made one…." The Smiths' children are back from college for the holiday weekend, I guess. The daughter, a freshman, proudly stands now instead of kneeling to receive. We didn't practice that in the training, but I'll wing it so she can demonstrate to her parents that she's attending a different kind of parish at college.

And there's Ken at last, who probably understands more than anyone how I feel about this moment. He looks up to meet my eyes as I say, "The blood of Christ." His "Amen" is not just to the communion, but to me. So be it. That's what I think too. "So from all lands thy Church be gathered…" Wipe and turn. "…into thy kingdom by thy Son."

Deliver us, when we draw near to thee, from coldness of heart and wanderings of mind.

BCP 833

When we human beings begin projects, we often do so with a fair amount of idealism. In the case of entering into a new ministry, this idealism can take the form of expecting that our work will supply one spiritual high after another. Somehow we convince ourselves that this part of church life will miraculously be exempt from the annoyances of the rest of church life. That here we will be peaceful and centered and full of gratitude for the presence of God. We will love everybody. Things will be different this time.

Perhaps given the awe some of us associate with the sanctuary, this unrealistic optimism may be a special hazard for LEMs. Just being there behind the altar rail can feel awesome—and if it does, make sure you thank God for letting you experience that feeling, as long as it lasts. The truth is that yes, it is awesome. If our subjective experience could be counted on to reflect objective reality, serving at God's altar would always make you feel that way.

But it won't. Our subjective experience is notoriously fickle; great teachers of prayer from every tradition have been warning us of this ever since people started praying. Just because God is awesome does not guarantee that you will get to feel awed. In fact, any LEM will tell you that there are times when you will feel exactly the opposite.

For example, you will probably discover an annoying mannerism to which your priest is prone. At close range, something as small as the way she hands you the chalice can begin to bother you. Or it may be his irrational refusal to consume, or his irrational insistence on consuming, the leftover wine all by himself, no matter how much there is.

You will also, sooner or later, lose patience with some of the congregants whom you are supposed to be serving in love. It may be those people who, waiting to intinct, seem deliberately to hide the host in their hands just to confuse you. It may be the communicants whose giant hats block your view of chalice placement, or those who expect you to pour the wine accurately into their mouths with no help.

So what do you do when the awe gives way to annoyance? Actually, admitting your annoyance (as your annoyance rather than as someone else's idiocy) is half the battle. Smiling at it helps. Mentioning the experience in general terms to someone you trust can release tension. There are various prayer avenues, too. Sometimes I ask for God's perspective on the individual who is driving me nuts. Sometimes I ask God to help me remember how utterly annoying I must be to all kinds of people. Other times I ask for a bigger insight, that this would help me get the idea that life is not of my design, and that it will inevitably take shapes that clash with my preferences.

And now and again, when I'm feeling really honest, I tell God that I would like a little taste of the awe again, please, just to help me remember why I'm here.

Let no evil talk come out of your mouths, but only what is useful for building up, as there is need, so that your words may give grace to those who hear.

Ephesians 4:29

There are people in the church who love to criticize, who (you can sometimes slip into thinking) seemingly come to church in order to increase the number of their opportunities to criticize. Because you are visible in a public role, you may begin to find yourself the target of their remarks. "Didn't anyone ever tell you not to wear brown shoes with vestments?" "You shouldn't put earrings on when you're serving at the altar." "My child never got the bread." And so on.

It hurts to be criticized for any reason. And it can hurt as well simply to find out how much criticism and negativity may be going on in your parish. Some criticisms, however, have much more to do with the individuals who offer them than with their targets. Learning to identify when this is the case will help you react in a more measured way.

But there can also be criticisms that are more obviously significant and potentially helpful. Maybe you are tipping the cup too far or not far enough. If you are unusually tall or unusually short, average-sized communicants may have to stretch or bend down to reach the chalice you are offering them. Some LEMs rush the words of administration slightly. If you could improve in areas like this, you'd want to, wouldn't you? And how would you know what needs improvement unless someone tells you?

Learning to receive healthy, constructive criticism will make it easier not to be blown off course by the other kind. In fact, some people even find it helpful just to ask for some constructive criticism. Find a few parishioners with no axes to grind and tell them you would like feedback the next time you serve. Is there anything they noticed that could have gone better? Was it easy and smooth to take a sip of wine from the chalice you held? Could they hear you?

The first time you listen to this kind of evaluation, it may feel dicey and embarrassing. ("You mean I've been practically choking people for six months and no one ever said anything?") Your initial response may be to defend yourself or blame the person who trained you. But you can let that response arise and notice it without giving it control over what you do. You can take the comments into God's presence with you and ask for help in receiving what is good and leaving the rest.

Talk that is useful for building up, as Ephesians calls it, will give grace. So if a criticism can be used to help you grow, if the act of learning to hear feedback can help open your own heart, then there is grace to be had from it. If a criticism is simply baseless and useless, finding something positive in the experience may be tricky. Still, it's possible. The grace in criticism, like the grace in most things, will often expand to fit the openness of your reaction.

On the contrary, the members of the body that seem to be weaker are indis-
pensable, and those members of the body that we think less honorable we
clothe with greater honor, and our less respectable members are treated
with greater respect.

1 Corinthians 12:22–23

About twenty-five minutes from my home a monastic community sits quietly on a hill. Even though I know none of its members personally, I've gotten in the habit of dropping by now and again to sit in the abbey church. I enjoy the building's stunning use of sunlight, but most of all I love to soak up the prayed-in feeling of the simple, powerful space.

The other day I arrived, it turned out, just as a period of eucharistic exposition was about to begin. I slid quickly into a pew and knelt as a stooped-over monk arranged the elements. Despite the sun streaming through a central skylight, he was wearing an unkempt, three-quarter length raincoat over his long black habit. Draped around his shoulders was a frayed strip of narrow purple cloth—someone's old stole, I suddenly realized, except that it hung half atop the rumpled raincoat and half under it.

The monk shuffled to the altar, closed the monstrance with an awkward clank, and set it down noticeably off center. After a quick hoisting of his body onto and off of its knees, he pivoted abruptly and headed for a pew, reminding me so irresistibly of an old television detective (raincoat and all) that I immediately christened him "Brother Columbo."

Doesn't every Christian community have one? And not just monasteries but parishes as well? It may not be public sloppiness that distinguishes the Brother or Sister Columbo in your parish, but there is, almost certainly, someone attending your church because she fits in nowhere else. Christian communities seem to attract people with eccentricities, differences, and uniquenesses.

And why not? Whether what makes someone different is chosen or hereditary, a curse or a blessing, isn't it our role as Christ's representatives to welcome all the weaker members of the body? There are so many places in this world where one has to squeeze oneself into a shape formed by someone else's demands. Everywhere we go, conditions seem to be placed on our acceptability. The dress code is posted quite clearly, sir. I'm sorry, but you'll have to show your membership card before we can admit you.

Is it any wonder people who can't make it into the mold eventually end up at church, lured by the claim that we follow a misfit Carpenter? We can prove them right quite easily: Turn to Brother Columbo and invite him just to come on in and be who he is, and that will be fine with everybody, thanks.

The apostles gathered around Jesus, and told him all that they had done and taught. He said to them, "Come away to a deserted place all by yourselves and rest a while."

Mark 6:30–31

There are predawn Sundays when my alarm goes off and I roll over, thinking that of all the possible activities that might fill this morning, here is the one that occupies the absolute bottom slot on the list: showing up at my parish, presiding, preaching, and being a priest to the people. At moments like that, I feel as if anything would be preferable to church. I'd rather fill out tax forms. I'd certainly rather stay in bed.

But I never do. I always get up, grind the coffee, eat some cereal, sit and gaze out the front windows. And by the time I arrive at church, my attitude has changed. The LEM for the eight o'clock service greets me, we light candles and arrange Prayer Books, I hear the floorboards begin to creak under the footsteps of faithful parishioners, and I want nothing more than to be there. It is meet and right so to do.

We all have times of distaste for our labors in the house of the Lord. This is normal, and they usually pass. But sometimes the moments of distaste come too often. They can string together into a season of exhaustion, when you feel as if your work is meaningless, your parish is declining, and the whole religion thing is probably false anyway. If you belong to a smaller church, there may be the added burden of thinking, "They'll never be able to find anyone else to do this job."

Here is what you should do at that point. Step down. Not forever, most likely, but until the burnout passes. Give up LEMing for Lent, and just go to worship. Sit and stand and kneel with your community, and let their prayer carry you. Plenty of time to give later. For now, receive.

Or maybe, at this point, church is the last place you need to be. When I am beginning to dry up spiritually, I find that an afternoon off, with no explicit "spirituality," can be restorative. A walk by the ocean, an hour's worth of poetry, big-city people-watching, singing along with an old Beatles album—all of these have helped refresh my spirit. Your refreshment may look very different, but it begins by asking: Where do you feel the most connected to life, the most yourself? Go there. What activity engages you so deeply that the hours slip away? Do that.

The reality is that most of us love our work for the church. But when we lose touch with that reality, there's something about other activities and places we also love that sets us right again. Periods of boredom and distaste are inevitable; burnout needn't be. If you know your loves, you have the resources to help prevent it.

But all things should be done decently and in order.

QUESTION AUTHORITY: It's a bumpersticker I haven't seen in a while. But for whatever reason that slogan has fallen into disuse, it's not because modern people have regained our trust in authority. We live in an age that is suspicious of anyone's seeming to be in charge, that encourages a low-key, "we're all just folks here" attitude.

While this relaxed attitude has a lot to recommend it, liturgy presumes authority. Not so that someone can order others around, but so that, as Paul suggests, things may come out decently and in order. Good liturgy has a measured lightness to it that often inspires comparisons to ballet. Everyone has his or her own steps to take in making the whole more effective and more beautiful.

Once I was in the sacristy of a seminary chapel before a Eucharist at which a recent graduate, an outgoing and dependable young woman, was to preside. Assigned as assisting clergy on the rota that day happened to be one of the institution's most venerable professors, an erudite priest approaching retirement. He had probably taught her everything she knew.

One might have expected this professor to take charge of the situation, to give his student a few helpful orders. In the eyes of the world, she owed deference to his age, his status, and (some might say) his gender. Yet the opposite happened. The scholar waited quietly to one side, graciously deferring to her as the day's celebrant, and, when she was ready, asked politely whether she had any special preferences for how he carried out the tasks that had been assigned to him.

Yes, liturgy presumes authority, but it is not the world's kind of authority. Liturgical authority does not rest on being bigger or smarter or richer or louder than the next guy. Liturgical authority is a light, free thing that lasts as long as the service does and is totally dependent on which of the many diverse roles you are playing today. Blurring this diversity—say, letting only LEMs read the lessons, or having the celebrant lead the Prayers of the People—can throw us back on other sources of authority, most of them more heavy-handed and less liberating.

When we stop conceiving of authority as permanent and intrinsic, we cast aside the world's terms. If we dare to let the liturgy itself locate us, we'll find that it locates us on one level only: those who play roles in the liturgy. By being assigned a role, you are empowered for that role, whatever it may be. And for the next hour or so, other sources of empowerment are not open to you. The assembled congregation, the LEMs, the cantor, the acolytes, the celebrant are all on level ground.

Equal in honor, one in Christ, given roles to play that match our gifts, we gather as one body doing all things decently and in order, but with a measured lightness and a flexible joy. Come ready to dance.

KNOCKING ON
THE DOOR

A wandering Aramean was my ancestor; he went down into Egypt and lived there as an alien, few in number, and there he became a great nation, mighty and populous.

Deuteronomy 26:5b

When I first tried to arrange a home communion with Ellen, she thought I was from the phone company and complained to me at length about repeated prank calls. An elderly member of the parish in failing health, Ellen probably had not stepped inside our building in ten years. Yet as soon as she became convinced that I genuinely came from "her church," she warmed to telling me stories of Episcopal Church Women meetings, parish suppers, long-ago auctions. She loved displaying her connections with the community I was there to represent.

Shut-ins, as we all too peremptorily call them, are a wealth of history, an archive of the parish life. Ask a question or two, and then just sit back and marvel. You will probably learn interesting and inspiring things: how admirably the ladies' guilds banded together for mutual support during the war; where the purple hangings really came from; who argued with whom over rebuilding the stairs to the parish hall. You may even discover that something that sounds eerily like the rector's latest creative programmatic initiative was being done every week in the 1940s.

By visiting an elderly member of the parish, we trace back into our own communal past. We learn to see ourselves in that most biblical way, as members of a community called by God. It is as if you have been given one end of a rope and keep following it hand over hand toward the other end, discovering more and more about your history. This is me, except I wasn't born then.

When I left Ellen's home that day, she wrote down my name and the name of the church on a piece of paper. It was funny to see the two next to each other like that, and I suspected that the slip of paper would lie on the table for quite a while, next to a forgotten invitation or a cup of tea. Perhaps when I come back it will still be there. Or perhaps Ellen will pick the paper up, read it, and be reminded of a ladies' guild meeting, imagining in her confusion that I was there with her. On the other hand, maybe I was.

Redeem the time; its hours too swiftly fly. The night draws nigh.

Hymn 541

Some of us are chronically late, and some chronically early. I grew up with a father who was the former and a mother who was the latter. My dad thought that if your plane was leaving at eight o'clock, you should be pulling out of the driveway for the airport at right about, oh, say, eight o'clock. Most of our family vacations began with a hysterical sprint to a distant departure gate. My mother, on the other hand, allowed for every possible delaying factor, gave the appearance of utter precision, and left us killing half hours in the parking lot before we could decently show up at events.

Chronically early people will be dismayed to discover that you cannot control all the circumstances surrounding home visits. Eventually, you will be late for one. The scheduled hour of arrival will come and go as you sit in traffic, or something you expected to take fifteen minutes will require forty-five. If you're going to be late, do try and call. If you don't know the number, call the church and get them to phone the person's house for you.

If you're going to be early, on the other hand, you have a gift of time being given to you. Usually, there is not enough of it to do anything that society would count as productive, like going to the ATM or the grocery store. (I tend to get about six minutes.) But there is enough for one thing. So don't just turn on the radio and fiddle with the station "seek" function as you drive around the block. Here is your chance to pray before the visit. Pull over.

It's all right. Gawkers will not stare at you. The police will not arrive. I've done "chronically early" car prayers in cemetery entrances, vacant lots, scenic overlooks, mall parking areas, and a few other places besides. So far, there has never been a negative consequence. Go ahead, try it.

It may be easiest to have a policy on what kind of prayer you will use for this specific occasion; if you have to carry on an interior debate as to whether you should open up your BCP to a psalm, say the Our Father, try and sing that new hymn you liked, just talk to God, or maybe do that technique they were teaching at the quiet day, your six minutes will be up and you'll never have started.

My own practice is to listen to an interior prayer word, which after years of use now signals to me that it is time simply to be attentive to God's presence. I could just as easily plan to intercede conversationally for the person I am about to see and for our visit, or to recite a memorized prayer. The policy is intended only to make sure that you actually pray, instead of just debating some plans about praying.

Six minutes may not be enough to find an ATM and make that transfer, but it's worth plenty in God's economy. When you redeem those little pieces of time, you'll see how much. What will your redemption policy be?

You have laid me in the depths of the Pit, in dark places, and in the abyss.
                                                              Psalm 88:7 (BCP)

Most often, home communions are warmly appreciative, chatty, and enjoyable. However, if you visit many people who are in pain, you will find that a friendly demeanor is not always enough. It is not an easy thing to offer yourself as a representative of Christ and his church to a suffering human being.

People may demand, in voices shaking with rage, that you explain their pain, that you justify the ways of God to them. While you will probably be tempted to try, it is very likely that the last thing they actually want to hear from you is an intellectual answer, a ready rationale for suffering. Polite twentieth-century humans usually don't scream and howl when guests are present; we express our pain verbally, and it comes out sounding like this: "How could God let this happen to me?" "Am I being punished?" "What has gone wrong with this damned world?"

I know how it feels to hear such questions, and I also know how it feels to howl them. Some time ago I underwent a shocking betrayal by an intimate prayer companion, after which I had to reconstruct much of my spiritual life. During this process, nothing was guaranteed to enrage me more than well-wishers whose "support" translated into neat religious platitudes. "God sent you this experience to help you appreciate other people's pain." "If that's the kind of person your friend was, you should be praising God for saving you from wasting any more time on him." One Christian to whom I unveiled my agony even ventured, "Well, when life gives you lemons, make lemonade."

After the pain was gone, I could begin to look at how God had been working for redemption even during a troubled person's unconscionable behavior. Now I can see ways in which evil became transformed into grace, and I can genuinely say thank-you for all God did for me that year. But while I was hurting, that kind of talk only made me hurt more.

So I am a lot more cautious now about trying to answer questions about suffering. I always show people that I have heard their lament, and I always honor whatever feelings they express. I tell them that there is much that even Christians just cannot answer. I say that we believe that God is with them somehow, even if it doesn't feel that way. Often I'll mention that since Jesus himself was "a man of sorrows, and acquainted with grief," we know that God understands and even suffers alongside us.

And the thing I say more than anything else is "tell Christ about it." I told him a thousand times, and he never turned me away. I called him every name in the book. Prayer is ultimately about being totally honest with God. If you can help a hurting person begin to do that, you have given the most valuable response of all.

When Jesus came to the place, he looked up and said to him, "Zacchaeus, hurry and come down; for I must stay at your house today." So he hurried down and was happy to welcome him. All who saw it began to grumble and said, "He has gone to be the guest of one who is a sinner."

Luke 19:5–7

Jesus had to look up that day because Zacchaeus, one of Jericho's high-ranking tax collectors, was sitting in a tree. He had climbed its branches to view Jesus' entourage for two reasons: First, he was short; and second, he was less than popular, I suspect, with the crowd thronging that street in Jericho. Zacchaeus was no patriarch, no wise man; I doubt anyone considered his home a "spiritual" place. Yet Jesus invited himself right on over: "Zacchaeus, I must stay at your house today."

Apparently, Zacchaeus was delighted. But not everyone would be. Some people are much more comfortable dressing up and going to Jesus' place than having him drop by theirs. When you call to set up a home communion appointment for Sunday, they'll hesitate.

It really isn't about you. They just feel odd receiving communion when the paten is sitting on a TV tray or a side table. They don't like seeing the daily newspaper lying so close to the corporal. They associate communion with church, naturally enough, and expect it to be accompanied by Bemberg damask, quiet organ music, and dark woodwork.

Perhaps you understand these feelings. It may take a while for you to get used to the difference in atmosphere as well. However, you will find that some of the holiest moments in your life can come when you welcome Christ into an unaccustomed place. Those rolling hospital tables, in particular, make marvelous altars. But anything does, really, when Jesus is there.

Whenever I take communion to someone who has never received outside of church before, I usually comment to them on how many different places Jesus went to be with people, and on how glad he must feel to be with us in this place now. After all, whatever holiness you treasure at church is really his, isn't it? Whatever atmosphere you love is meant to point to Christ. And now, whoever you are, whatever people think, Jesus himself has come right here to be with you. Sure, it's messy, and there are unpaid bills on the table, weighted down by that glass with the dried-up orange juice on the bottom. Sure, you're no matriarch or patriarch. But open up, Zacchaeus, because he wants to stay at your house today.

THE REST OF
THE WEEK

*The ministry
of lay persons
is to represent
Christ and his
Church; to
bear witness to
him wherever
they may be;
and, according
to the gifts
given them, to
carry on
Christ's work
of reconcilia-
tion in the
world; and to
take their place
in the life, wor-
ship, and gov-
ernance of the
Church.*

BCP 855

M y fingerprint is on the chalice, but my hands touch a lot of other things during the week, too. If I am supposed to represent Christ at the rail, if I am supposed to be one link in this great chain of witnesses, I can't just do that on Sundays at the service. I have to do it elsewhere in my life.

The Prayer Book describes the ministry of the laity in some detail, but interestingly enough, the *last* thing mentioned in its list is what goes on in church. Before you are a LEM, you are a witness-bearer, a reconciler, someone who represents Christ in the world. In fact, the Prayer Book says that "to represent Christ and his Church" is the primary ministry of all of us, lay or ordained. That same phrase shows up right down the line in the catechism. Laity, bishop, priest, deacon—God calls each of us, above all else, to represent Christ and his Church.

So your ministry, at its root, is the same as the ministry of, say, the bishop of your diocese. The difference between you and your bishop is how and in what context God calls you to carry out that ministry.

"To represent Christ and his Church." When you think about it, there may not be much choice on this one. Whether or not you consciously decide to label your activities as a representation of Christ, people will associate you with your parish—particularly now that you have taken on a ministry as visible as being a LEM. If you are "that man who chewed out the attendant at the gas station" or "that woman who never puts out her recycling bin," others may take your behavior as a statement of what Episcopalians—or even Christians in general—are like.

To represent Christ. This doesn't mean being prudish or a Pollyanna; in fact, Jesus was certainly neither. But it means at least that whether you are at the rail or in the mall, you have to be the same person. Your ministry doesn't begin when you show up fifteen minutes early on Sunday and stop when the vestments come off for coffee hour. It began before you had even noticed it, and it's *always* going on.

But whenever you pray, go into your room and shut the door and pray to your Father who is in secret; and your Father who sees in secret will reward you.
Matthew 6:6

When I was going through college, I had some friends who seemed to seek out opportunities to discuss their "morning quiet times." My suspicion was that they were intentionally targeting these remarks for my benefit. Hearing their enthusiasm, surely I would soon fall into line and start waking up for Bible study every day before going to the cafeteria.

The discipline these friends had was admirable but, while I did dutifully admire them, they mostly made me feel guilty. And it wasn't as if I was an inactive Christian either. I prayed with some kind of regularity. I read spiritual books. I worshiped in church most Sundays and several Fridays. But I didn't have a "morning quiet time," and that's what my friends said counted the most.

A similar guilt used to surface later, when spiritually serious Episcopalians would tell me that of course the Anglican tradition assumed that one ought to read Morning and Evening Prayer each day. A different context, but the same prescription: Pray the way we say, or you're hardly praying at all.

Perhaps nobody has ever blamed you for not having a set quiet time or for not reading the Office, but surely you've heard someone hold a particular practice up as being the hallmark of a good Christian's personal devotional life. If you really meant it, you would be doing this.

Obviously, having some prayer practice outside of church is an important thing, but it has to fit you. It has to flow from your spirituality and not from somebody else's. And if it is motivated by guilt, you will sabotage yourself before long and stop doing it anyway.

When I finally gave up on prayer-time guilt, I decided to follow my spiritual instincts and see where they led me. And ironically enough, I have ended up with a morning quiet time that includes the Daily Office. But this practice became possible and authentic only very gradually, piece by piece. I pray the Office now not because other Episcopalians say I should, but because I have grown to love it so deeply that I can barely even imagine living without it.

A modern monk used to give people this very wise advice: "Pray as you can, not as you can't." How can you pray these days? If you know the answer, put the book down and do it. If you don't know the answer, put the book down and find out.

We humbly pray you so to guide and govern us by your Holy Spirit, that in all the cares and occupations of our life we may not forget you.

BCP 100

Each morning I receive an Internet e-mail message that contains a thought for the day from a Christian spiritual writer. Sometimes the editor for this service will also include a short prayer based on the passage. The other day that prayer was designed to be repeated with each in-breath and out-breath: "In all I do… gentleness." Sitting in front of the computer monitor, I breathed, "In all I do… gentleness." What a lovely sentiment. Certainly worth aspiring to. I felt briefly pleased to be a person who gives attention to the things of the Spirit, even if only for a second or two before work.

The day was a tough one. A workshop to write, a person who scheduled time with me at the last minute and then failed to show up, a doctor's appointment that broke the most productive part of the day in half, a still unfinished sermon, and, to top it off, ecclesiastical guests coming for dinner. Having arrived home in the late afternoon, I was putting away the previous night's dishes. Well, to be a little more forthcoming about it, I was slamming the previous night's dishes into their cabinets as loudly as possible, hoping that the racket might assist the other occupant of the house in recognizing how greatly I was being inconvenienced by the insurmountable difficulties of my uniquely grueling existence. Maybe he'd even offer to cook. And then, just as two lids banged together on the way to the shelf, there it was. "In all I do... gentleness."

I had to laugh. First at my own total lack of gentleness at that point, and second, at my half-conscious morning assumption that breathing in front of a computer monitor for a minute could suffice to set an enduring spiritual tone for the next eight hours.

Of course, many people read a brief meditation each day. You're doing it now, for example. But time for the Spirit somehow needs to overflow its boundaries and soak into our daily decisions and tasks. It needs a different kind of openness than what we are able to give during a run through the morning e-mail, before sprinting to the next urgent activity.

"In all I do... gentleness" was a fine thought for the day. However, thinking it once and checking it right off the to-do list gave it little opportunity to have an effect on me. I needed a way to keep gentleness at hand. Maybe I could have stopped for reflection during the day, asking how gentle was this or that action. Or I could have copied the original passage onto a card and tucked it in my date book. There are any number of possibilities. Come to think of it, just saying the prayer the way it was intended would have been a good start.

Open, O LORD, the eyes of all people to behold thy gracious hand in all thy works, that, rejoicing in thy whole creation, they may honor thee with their substance, and be faithful stewards of thy bounty.

BCP 329

Sooner or later every Episcopalian hears about stewardship—especially in October or thereabouts, when too often it is a code word for pledging. ("Please do your part to fund next year's budget. You receive many benefits from your membership here; we need your help to keep providing them.") This may be thoughtful fund-raising, but it is not stewardship. It sounds more like an expectation placed on the members of a club: In order to belong, you must support the annual banquet by (a) an in-kind donation, (b) volunteering so much time the weekend of the event, or (c) making a financial contribution.

Stewardship, on the other hand, works the opposite way. It begins from noticing that God has given you everything you have. If you doubt this, reflect for a minute: Who gave you life in the first place? Who gave you the environment that has produced your talents and fostered your training? Who gave you the energy that has allowed you to pursue success? Who is holding you in being at this very moment? Stewardship asks: How much of what has come to you as a gift do you need to pass along in order to be spiritually healthy? Being a steward means managing all the gifts God gave you—time, talent, treasure—in dialogue with God.

As a LEM, for example, you are already practicing stewardship of those resources every time you serve. You are giving back a percentage of what God has given you in the areas of time and talent. But of course there is more time in your week than just Sunday mornings. There are more talents within you that can do God's work in other arenas. And of course there's whatever money God has given you, with all the work it can do.

Many people grudgingly inquire about how much of their resources they have to donate to the church. But when you take on the outlook of a steward, you may find yourself asking the opposite question: What proportion of God's gifts can you justifiably keep for yourself? Giving back to God with this attitude can help you to become more generous, less controlling, and less anxious about grasping what is "yours." If you are becoming a giving person, you may find yourself allowing your hands to relax and spread outward in trust, opening to God and to the world. And then who knows what riches might pass through them?

He has told you, O mortal, what is good; and what does the LORD require of you but to do justice, and to love kindness, and to walk humbly with your God?

Micah 6:8

Not many parishes encourage those volunteering in the liturgy to consider themselves excused from volunteering for other projects—most notably, outreach. Anyone who reads the Bible will notice its frequent references to our responsibility for the poor and outcast. In fact, some people would argue that unless we involve ourselves somehow in the cause of social justice, our service to Christ is incomplete.

If that perspective inspires you to show up at, say, the local soup kitchen, one of your early discoveries will be that you have mixed motives. When giving, we usually do. In our hearts, there is one voice that speaks unselfishly, sincerely appreciating the needs and perspectives of the people we serve. It moves us to listen before we act. It says: They could be you, you know. But most of us also hear another interior voice that is less admirable. It prompts us to think more of our own generosity than of others' reality. It writes secret spin-doctor headlines about "My Benevolence to the Needy." It says: You are not like them, the poor dears.

Whenever I ask people to notice that second voice, I remember a couple from the homeless shelter where I worked in the 1980s, and I think of how gracefully they once responded to it. Leanne and Chuck were in their forties and a familiar part of the street scene in town. Chuck had served a prison term for a crime of which he freely admitted he was guilty, but since meeting Leanne he had mellowed and turned thoughtful.

One warm summer evening the two of them meandered in the side door of the shelter carrying paper plates, which turned out to be laden with chicken. Looking at the odd cast of their faces, I wondered briefly if the couple had crashed a local picnic. Then they surprised me further by quietly depositing the plates in the nearest trash can.

"Hey, Leanne, where'd you guys get that stuff?" I cautiously inquired.

It was Chuck who answered, explaining in a bemused tone, "This BMW pulled up out front and rolled down the windows, so I went to ask what they wanted. They stuck these plates out at us and the guy said, 'We couldn't finish our supper tonight. Would you like it?'"

My Benevolence to the Needy. Outrage rose as I felt the insult on Chuck's behalf, and I snapped, "Why didn't you throw it in his face?"

"Oh, I don't know," murmured Chuck. He paused, looked at Leanne, and then simply said, "I figured he just needed to feel good about himself."

Now, take a look at those two men together. On the "acceptable" side of society, a wealthy do-gooder congratulated himself for passing table scraps to the poor; on the "unacceptable" side, an insightful street person freely chose to allow a BMW liberal his illusions. So answer this: Who was the generous one?

In him, you have delivered us from evil, and made us worthy to stand before you. In him, you have brought us out of error into truth, out of sin into righteousness, out of death into life.

BCP 368

If we dare believe these words we say, our whole way of thinking can get reframed in church. It won't happen every week, but it does happen sometimes. We create the community of God together and savor a foretaste of the kingdom. We discover ourselves as characters in a cosmic story, one that relativizes whatever prejudices and theories we walked in with. Standing together around the altar, we are located at the center of God's world, and it seems for a moment that we see as God sees.

When we have such a time of vision around the altar, it is meant to lead us into that vision for the rest of the week. If we include everyone here, why aren't we doing it outside? Why are there no women or people of color on the board of directors? If we take an attitude of servanthood here, why don't we do it at home? Why do I resent reaching over to pass my companion the sugar on Monday morning?

What radical truths we affirm together at every Eucharist—and, so often, how poorly we follow through on them. We joyously proclaim that Christ has redeemed creation, and yet we easily turn defeatist and glum. We gratefully announce that God forgives, and yet we place all kinds of conditions on our own forgiveness. The trust we express here is so ultimate that you would think that we'd be strangers to anxiety. But let us get back to the office, and we are so anxious that we are paging and dialing and faxing all at the same time, with a breathless determination to run everything ourselves.

Sometimes I wonder if we even read our own stuff. When we say "out of error into truth, out of sin into righteousness, out of death into life," we are making a proclamation that should mean something not only within the walls of our church but outside them as well. We are shouting, against all the voices that tell us otherwise, that there is a different way to live. We are affirming, against all the voices that say the real story is death and dehumanization, that no story ends there. Like peace-loving protesters facing the tanks of a totalitarian state, we are standing for truth in a strange land.

"Out of error into truth, out of sin into righteousness, out of death into life." Take it beyond the church walls, and I'll tell you this much: We shall overcome.

PRAYING ON THE WAY

Prayers for the Use of
Lay Eucharistic Ministers

Before Serving
Here I am, Lord. There are many reasons I am here, but this is the real one: I have come because you called me. I offer myself and my time and my gifts to serve that call. Use me today for your glory and for the welfare of your people, through Jesus Christ our savior. Amen.

After Serving
Thank you, God, for your indescribable gifts. Whether or not I felt your presence, you have been with me. Whether or not I came away satisfied with the job I did, your love is enough for me. As I leave this place, do not let me forget you. Come with me everywhere, and make my words and deeds into part of the leaven of the kingdom. In Jesus' name, Amen.

A Traditional Prayer after the Holy Eucharist
Blessed, praised, worshiped, and adored be Jesus Christ on his throne in heaven, in the sacrament of the altar, and in the hearts of his faithful people forevermore.

Breath Prayers to Use during the Liturgy or at Other Times
Any appropriate sentence from Scripture or other text can be made into a prayer to be offered with each in-breath and out-breath. While it is best to set aside special times to

focus only on your breath prayer, you can also pray this way at idle moments, while doing repetitive work, or as a background during worship services.

With use, the sentence you choose will often gradually and naturally edit itself, dividing into two rhythmic units and perhaps losing some nonessential words. For example, "Create in me a clean heart, O God, renew a right spirit within me" could become "create a clean heart/ renew a right spirit," even "clean heart/ right spirit" or "create, O God/ renew, O God." Some people enjoy experimenting in this way; others prefer to ask God to give them a breath prayer that is right for them. Here are a few more examples of such prayers:

Perfect love/ casts out fear.
Be known to us, Lord Jesus/ in the breaking of the bread.
Lord, have mercy/ Christ, have mercy.
Lord, I believe/ Help my unbelief.
Bless the Lord/ O my soul.
Abide in me/ and I in you.

A Collect for Meditation

Any Christian text may serve for meditation if you simply pray it very slowly, word by word or concept by concept. The ancients used to compare this kind of prayer to a cow chewing its cud; ruminate over each idea as long as it goes on speaking to you. When there seems to be no more nourishment to be drawn from a word, go on to the next one. It is possible to spend a whole afternoon praying through an Epistle in this way, or you can set aside a briefer time to meditate on a shorter text. Here is an example that is especially appropriate for LEMs:

God our Father, whose Son our Lord Jesus Christ in a wonderful Sacrament has left us a memorial of his passion: Grant us so to venerate the sacred mysteries of his Body and Blood, that we may ever perceive within ourselves the fruit of his redemption; who lives and reigns with you and the Holy Spirit, one God, for ever and ever. Amen.

BCP 252